THE BOOK OF MOSES

SURVIVING CHILDHOOD TRAUMA

MOSES MATTOX
AS TOLD TO: ROSS WILLIAMS

Copyright 2024 by Moses Mattox

All rights reserved. No part of this publication may be reproduced, distributed, or transmitted in any form or by any means, including photocopying, recording, or other electronic or mechanical methods, without the prior written permission of the author or publisher, except in the case of brief quotations embodied in critical reviews and certain other noncommercial uses permitted by copyright law. For permission requests regarding this story, contact the author or publisher. Printed in the United States of America.

ISBN: 979-8-9906181-0-7

First Printing, 2024

Author

IG: @kingmoses_85

FB & TikTok: Moses Mattox

Publisher

Williams Commerce, LLC

IG | Twitter | Facebook: @wcwriting1

Visit Our Website: Williamscommerce1.com

Table of Contents

Chapter 1: Drinking Partner 1

Chapter 2: Invisible Roaches 7

Chapter 3: My Mom's "Friend" 13

Chapter 4: Departed Soul 17

Chapter 5: Warning Shots 21

Chapter 6: Ransacked 23

Chapter 7: Trust Issues 27

Chapter 8: It'll Always Be Me & You 31

Chapter 9: He Had It Coming 33

Chapter 10: Nowhere To Go 35

Chapter 11: My First Crush 39

Chapter 12: Santa Claus 45

Chapter 13: The Fire Alarm 47

Chapter 14: Suspension 51

Chapter 15: Everlasting Whippings 57

Chapter 16: Trapped in Trauma 61

Chapter 17: Spike 62

Chapter 18: Steak and Shrimp 67

Chapter 19: Someone Please Call 911 71

Chapter 20: The First of The Month 73

Chapter 21: Broken Appliances 79

Chapter 22: Hit & Run 83

Chapter 23: LA Gears 87

Chapter 24: Flesh & Blood 91

Chapter 25: Fork in The Road 95

CHAPTER 1

Drinking Partner

I might be the only person on this earth whose first memories were drunk ones. It feels like the only thing in this world I haven't done is die. After overcoming what I will open up about in this book, I know for sure that I have a God-sent path.

This memoir isn't a struggle story. This book is a story about how I made it through the struggle to use my life as a testimony to impact others.

My life didn't develop a sense of normalcy until I first tasted alcohol. Too often in hoods across the world, young black children are growing up without a father. I was born to a 16 year old single mother in 1986.

Unless my father bears a striking resemblance to me, I wouldn't recognize him if we were sitting in the same room. He was out of my mother's life before she gave birth to his child. Therefore, only my maternal family exists to me.

Drinking Partner

My mother and two of my uncles, who became my father figures, were my grandmother's only children who weren't hooked on drugs. The crack era took out some of the best men and women of the culture. There were potential movie stars, professional athletes, and businesspeople in the hood who couldn't make it past their addictions and adversities. Eight of my aunts and uncles fell victim.

Father figures are a precious commodity. I know my Uncle Lenny cared for me. Since he was one of the only positive male figures in the family, he played the role of a father to many of his nieces, nephews, and cousins.

My Uncle Lenny would be the one to pull up when we needed discipline. Life often served as my form of discipline.

My mom was a woman of the streets. Because of her fighting skills and gorgeous looks, she earned the nickname Knockout. She was also a businesswoman ahead of her time. Her business on the streets kept her away from home, so my grandmother and uncle were the ones to step in when I needed coverage or scolding.

On one occasion, my uncle picked me up and told me he wouldn't be disciplining me once he saw the fear

Drinking Partner

in my eyes. Car rides with my uncle were one of the most feared activities in the family. A kid or a family member acting up would know they were in trouble when he pulled up. He would quietly approach the misbehaver and coldly say, "Come ride with me."

Once I would get in his car, he would tell me to sit in the middle back seat. During the first few blocks, he held long drawn-out conversations like in a gangster movie. The first few minutes would be quiet, then he asked, "Why did your mom have to call me to come get you?"

Several minutes later, he would break the silence and ask, "Do you think that was the right thing to do?" Not everyone would get to a third question.

After the second one, he'd reach across the back seat and punch me in my chest. Then start whaling off on me. I became so traumatized from these rides that I still don't sit in the middle back seat 30+ years later.

The more I cried, the worse the whippings got. I don't know what it was about this line that black elders from my era loved so much, "Stop crying before I give you something to cry for."

Drinking Partner

This always happened after there were multiple reasons to cry and the pain had already been inflicted. That was one of my uncle's favorite lines while he whipped me.

I thought he was doing me a favor during one occasion when he told me he wouldn't be whipping me this time. He told me to pretend like it happened. In retrospect, it may have been better for him to abuse me rather than what he did the next time he picked me up.

I did everything in my power to figure out why my uncle didn't discipline me this time when he was called to. There wasn't much power to exert at five years old. While I stared at him, he asked, "What are you looking at?"

It was the same thing all the cousins looked at when they got in the car. He drank and drove, more than he buckled up. He kept a pack of beer close to him and a beer in his right hand almost everywhere he went. When I didn't have a response to his question, he asked, "Do you want one?"

The opportunity to first impress my Uncle Lenny was when he handed me a beer at five years old, and I downed it like a middle-aged man after a hard day of

Drinking Partner

work. This was one of the first times it felt like I made someone proud. He encouraged me to join him in finishing the six-pack of beer, and then we stopped to get a 12-pack.

I was throwing up and had a head high, but my uncle appeared to be having the time of his life. When he dropped me off, he didn't tell my mom a thing, and I didn't either because I couldn't. I went straight to sleep.

I had an irrational desire to be under my uncle because my father was never a part of my life. Being affirmed by a man is a natural desire for a young boy. Becoming my uncle's drinking partner was my way of getting the affirmation I desired. At this point, I had become closer to him than his own children. Liquor became a coping mechanism for everything.

Imagine a second grader coping with a day of elementary school by drinking a beer. I could find alcohol anywhere or bribe someone to get it for me. Initially, I thought this would be a one-time occasion, but this began happening almost every time he picked me up. My uncle moved to a nearby town, but his addiction remained with me.

CHAPTER 2

Invisible Roaches

S elling crack was a prerequisite for an '80s queen pin. I didn't realize what my mother did for a living until the age of six. I just knew she would shower us with gifts and make sure we didn't go without. Providing this type of lifestyle without having to go to work made me curious.

My Uncle Henry and I got into everything together. We got into the worst thing possible once my mom and her boyfriend left us at home by ourselves. A unique dynamic in many inner-city families is uncles or aunts around the same age as their nieces or nephews. My Uncle Henry and I were eight years apart. He still leveraged that title when it was convenient for him.

My mom was so influential in the streets that she put her boyfriend on. He was a heavyweight boxer, but turned to the streets once he and my mom began hustling together. I saw him stash something in the top cabinet, then hurry out of the house to go somewhere with my mother. We assumed it was a special treat like

Invisible Roaches

white chocolate since they hid it so discreetly. However, it wasn't discreet enough to hide it from us.

After their rear lights disappeared in the distance, my brother and I hurried to the kitchen. We worked as a team to retrieve what he stashed. Henry and I were oblivious to what crack cocaine was at the time. We heard them talk about it on the news and in the neighborhood but hadn't been face-to-face with it until now.

Henry and I had a face and stomach filled with crack cocaine thirty seconds after opening the pack on the kitchen floor. The aftertaste of cocaine is one of the harshest tastes on earth. My mouth went numb immediately, but I kept eating the substance until it felt like invisible roaches were crawling on me. If you see anyone under the influence scratching themselves, more than likely, this is why they are scratching.

I saw invisible roaches with no antennas or bodies scrambling up and down my body after the crack infiltrated my system. Henry and my face were no longer there, only the invisible roaches.

My heart felt like it was about to pound holes in my chest while the cocaine increased my heart rate to

Invisible Roaches

hazardous levels. Being in the dark made things even scarier. I ran upstairs, fearing each moment in front of me.

Thankfully, my mom and her boyfriend weren't gone for long. They were frequently in and out of the house. I felt slightly relieved when I heard them enter the front door. As she made her way upstairs, I began thinking about the trouble I'd get into. This was the first time I felt extreme paranoia. I was worried about everything in the world as my mother neared me.

When my mom and her boyfriend returned, we were spooked and hurried upstairs. As soon as we made it to the top steps, her boyfriend yelled, "Why are these lights off?" and then flipped them back on. I instantly remembered the kitchen being a hot mess, like someone had broken in.

My pupils covered almost every millimeter of my eyes when my mom and I locked eyes. My eyelids may as well have been glued in opposite directions. I tried squinching them, but they wouldn't budge. The rest of my features were out of whack also. My mouth was cheesy, and my cheeks were spasming. My mom was so confused until she felt my chest.

Invisible Roaches

My brother's dad was knocking things over while my mom approached me. She repeatedly asked what was wrong with me until my brother's dad began cursing up a storm. Once they put two and two together, she started panicking like me. He began fussing at her while she was trying to find a solution for a six-year-old who consumed plenty of crack cocaine.

My grandmother was the person everyone called when they needed something. That's who my mom called first. Once my grandmother answered the phone she said, "Stop! Slow down! Don't call anyone else except for this number. If you do call someone else, you will go to jail, and they will take our kids!"

Drugs were so bad in the 80s and early 90s that there was a commonly called "poison hotline" to combat the effects of illegal substances. Once my mom called, she asked, "What should I do if I have a friend who accidentally consumed a lot of crack cocaine?"

The operator said, "Get your friend some milk immediately." My mother hung up the phone and then sped off to get her "friend" some milk.

Invisible Roaches

She returned with gallons of milk and force-fed me. Being lactose intolerant made the high even worse. My stomach was now a mess like my heart, head, and the rest of my mind and body.

My mom stuck her finger down my throat and that started an onslaught of me throwing up and milk shooting out of my nose. Before the sun came up, I had a seizure, along with non-stop shakes and jitters. I wasn't able to sleep, smile, or cry for two days.

I itched for a few weeks and was paranoid that the invisible roaches would return. I don't know if my mom was so frantic that she was one more wrong move from going to jail and having me taken away or because I was fighting for life after a crack overdose at the tender age of 6.

Either way, I was thankful to see her life-saving efforts. It felt like I was on the verge of dying while the cocaine pumped through my undeveloped system.

When I did lay down it couldn't be in my bed because I thought the invisible roaches were in there. It felt like I fell asleep before I even laid down that night. I slept for an entire day, but the symptoms

Invisible Roaches

lingered. On the bright side, no one would ever have to worry about me trying another drug again.

CHAPTER 3

My Mom's "Friend"

My childhood innocence was officially stripped away from me at the age of six. I tried suppressing this memory more than my unfortunate experience with crack cocaine. During a casual night at home, I fell asleep in the living room on the floor while my mother laid on the couch behind me.

We had a new TV set that sat on the floor and was a popular gathering spot. My brother, uncle, and mom's friend, Sharon, were in the living room also.

My mom's friend and I were the only two people still awake. Everyone that knows my mom, knows that she's a heavy sleeper. Sharon examined my mom to ensure she was asleep, then examined me for unforeseen reasons. I thought she was trying to help me out when she guided me down the hallway into a bedroom.

Once we got behind closed doors, she pulled out one of her breasts and asked me if I had ever seen one of these before. I instantly became uncomfortable, but

My Mom's "Friend"

I hadn't seen anything yet. My silence didn't deter the slender perverted woman.

When I didn't respond, she took my hand and told me to grab one. While one of her breasts sat in my hand, she used her hands to show me how to massage it. I don't know if my childishness toward sex or lack of consent turned her on, but Sharon acted even more in heat when she pulled me closer and made me get on top of her. She stripped down and only had a t-shirt on. My other hand was drawn back until she pulled it to the entryway of her vagina.

The foreplay went to another level when she started kissing and licking on me, then pulled my pants down to give me oral sex.

My eyes and hands tightened, and my toes curled but not from pleasure. There wasn't an enjoyable moment of being violated at such an early age. Sharon kept assuring me that it was okay when I questioned if it really was okay. I was forced to lose my virginity before I even knew what sex was.

Once my mom's friend finished kissing all over me, she laid on her back and told me to get on top of her.

My Mom's "Friend"

Without even the care to make sure I was protected, she made me penetrate her without a condom.

I was forced into the risk of contracting a sexually transmitted disease before I reached puberty. I was too young to conceptualize if this was right or wrong, but it didn't sit right with my spirit. I was under extreme discomfort and pressure. She moved my waist up and down to mimic stroking motions and made me give her oral sex while being suffocated.

My discomfort carried on to the next day. I couldn't carry on without letting someone know what happened to me. Emotional availability wasn't a thing in my family, and it felt like my mom was the only person I could turn to with a situation this sensitive.

We were at the projects near my grandmother's house. She was talking to someone when I couldn't resist the urge to tell her what happened. There wasn't urgency for her to hear what I had to say. She carried on to the next conversation while I followed her around trying to get her attention.

When my mom saw I wasn't going anywhere and got tired of me holding her back from a good time, I whispered in her ear what happened. I don't know if

My Mom's "Friend"

she was attempting to conceal her emotions in public or if she didn't believe me.

I expected her to show anger and look for her friend with vengeance on her mind. My mom kept a straight face when I told her about her friend molesting me, and that left me feeling unsettled. I couldn't confirm if my mom retaliated or not because we never spoke about it again and I never saw her friend again.

I wondered how hard my mother truly cut for me when she didn't respond how I expected to after she got the news I was molested. Was her friend more important than me? Did she do something to her? Or did she not believe me? To this day, I pray those questions don't go unanswered forever.

CHAPTER 4

Departed Soul

I experienced more tragedy by the age of 7 than most people do in a lifetime. Not too many gatherings during my upbringing ended with people peacefully going their separate ways. One get-together at my mother's house took a turn for the worse.

People were having the times of their lives smoking and drinking until my cousin Andre and Uncle Lenny got into it with a set of brothers over a video game. Terrell and Jerel terrorized the neighborhood and had long arrest records. One of the brothers had just gotten out of prison.

Days after getting released he was in my mother's living room cursing at the top of his lungs like he ran the house and paid the bills there. The disrespect infuriated my family. My uncle was the enforcer in our family and couldn't let anyone disrespect our tribe, especially at our house. The children usually hung out upstairs during gatherings while the adults remained downstairs and outside. I was that one nosey kid trying

Departed Soul

to get an understanding of everything that was going on.

Once I made it halfway down the steps and peeked through the wooden guardrail, the men in the living room started throwing hands. Sounds of fists banging on bodies sounded over the early 90s rap. After half of the living room had been damaged and several glasses shattered, the set of brothers sprinted out of the house, and my uncle and cousin ran after them.

The brothers lived one street over. My uncle went after one, and my cousin went after the other. The guy Andre chased was out of sight shortly after he started chasing him. I spotted my cousin as soon as he gave up. He walked down the side alley of the house with his head down until my grandmother and two other family members shouted his name.

Before Andre could look up, the guy he was chasing shot him twice in the back of the head. Once he collapsed to the ground, the assassin stood over my cousin and dumped bullets into him to ensure he was dead.

As my cousin's soul departed from the earth, my mom rushed me to the car and an aunt brought me to

Departed Soul

my grandmother's house. While we were hurried to the car, my uncle reappeared with his shirt off, crying and screaming our cousin's name as if his cries could bring him back.

People were already afraid of him, and he had a gun in his hand, but that didn't stop my grandmother from disarming and consoling him. The murderer went to jail, but a dark cloud remained over my family after my cousin's death.

CHAPTER 5

Warning Shots

Looking back on it, a considerable amount of my trauma could have been avoided by just listening. Some of it was inevitable, but not on this occasion.

My mom told me to stay in the house that day because something was rumored to go down at the rec center. Shortly after hanging out where I wasn't supposed to, my cousin Jerome bumped heads with an enemy who looked like he had a tough life. He couldn't have been older than 20, but he looked twice his age.

Jerome gained a reputation for making more enemies than friends. Plenty of people had problems with him. He messed with other men's girlfriends, talked to people disrespectfully, and committed armed robberies.

A guy my cousin had beef with said, "Man, I don't know who you think you are playing with, but I'll take your life right where you stand!"

Warning Shots

When he brandished a gun and pressed it against Jerome's temple, everyone ran. Before I could reach full speed, a shot rang out. Tears sprinkled the concrete while I sprinted home. I spent the rest of that day grieving.

My family had already been through enough. This was only months after losing Andre to gun violence. Jerome may have been terrorizing the streets, but we loved him deeply. I cried myself to sleep that night.

The following day, I found out that wasn't the end of his story. Jerome's enemy shot a revolver but missed his target. I almost fainted when my cousin reappeared the next day.

CHAPTER 6

Ransacked

At the age of 8, one of my hustles became breaking into stores. I had the key to the city, literally. I was in the third grade but I had a method of breaking into any deadbolt or safe. That skill made me fit right in with my family.

My family always had a hustle or scam going including forgery, burglary, and plenty of other forms of illegal entrepreneurship. They introduced me to burglarizing when I was 8.

My mom took me on a mission with several other relatives in the neighborhood. I had already proved that I was reliable, loyal, and agile. It was as if they were scouting me for a professional team. They knew I liked to climb trees and was a team player. For their plan to be executed, they needed someone my height.

I had no idea where we were going when my mother told me to take a ride with the family. After overhearing them talking, I assumed we were going to get some snacks or groceries. When we went to a closed

Ransacked

convenience store, my cousin helped me crawl into a window.

While I scaled down the wall as if I were Spiderman, they called for me to hurry up and unlock the front door. When I did, my family started ransacking the place. They started grabbing bottles of malt liquor, cartons of cigarettes, scratch-off tickets, and other non-essentials. While I watched them in dismay, one of my cousins yelled, "Grab some snacks!"

I would have aborted the mission if I knew this was how they were talking about getting snacks. Instead, I was lured into burglarizing. The rest of the neighborhood was lured into burglarizing also. They began looting the corner store after my family ransacked it.

My family took the hustle a step further when they started selling the stolen items throughout the city. In retrospect, some of them could have been world-renowned salespeople.

One cousin was so savvy with the sales, that he began running specials. He had one deal where a fiend would receive a free 40-ounce of malt liquor if they purchased a certain amount of crack. That was high-

Ransacked

level cross-promotion and marketing. I was always looking for the next lick to hit with them. I always learned something new and got the thrill of a lifetime.

Believe it or not, this was when things took a turn for the worse. As if they could get any more challenging, I started splitting time between my mother and grandmother's house. Neither was a sanctuary for peace which is what a household is supposed to be. Almost everyone in the family laid their heads at my grandmother's house. You would just have to find a space to sleep and get in where you fit in.

My mom's house started becoming the same way. She had a new boyfriend and a friend living with us. Her friend had two children near my age. The number of kids at our house mirrored the student body of a small daycare.

Our home was usually filled with unsupervised kids doing things they weren't supposed to be doing. My mom's boyfriend wasn't her type. Each man before had a certain toughness or street appeal to him. This guy was a dancer from New York and shied away from confrontation. He was no match for my mother. She wore the pants in that relationship and dictated

Ransacked

everything. Randy treated my mom as if she was out of his league. If my mom asked him to jump, he'd ask her how high. I didn't realize how chaotic things were in their relationship until a secret and life-changing event caused things to spiral out of control.

CHAPTER 7

Trust Issues

During one frigid day with heavy snow, my mom was gone for the day. This was common, but the rest of the day wasn't.

Most of the kids were playing downstairs where we typically weren't allowed. My mother's boyfriend and her friend thought that all the kids were downstairs. While they assumed they were all alone I witnessed them having sex. Only her friend saw me, but that didn't stop her. She and my mom's boyfriend continued having sex after I ran away.

You should never discount why a person has trust issues. You never know what they have seen. How could I trust so freely when I watched my mom put a roof over a woman's head, and she still slept with her man?

I didn't spend much time contemplating if I should tell my mom. It appeared that I was her only real friend. One of her close friends molested me, and the other had sex with her man.

Trust Issues

This encounter made me permanently suspicious of almost everyone in her life. Consequently, I was beyond suspicion with Randy. I knew where he stood and what type of man he was.

I ratted on Randy as soon as my mother made it home that night. There was no way I could betray her like he did. My mom had more questions about her man cheating than when I got molested. I didn't have to spend much time convincing her. I was known for demonstrating what I discussed.

Regardless of my juvenile encounter with sex, I couldn't make up for what I demonstrated and saw. My mom knew there was validity to what I said, so she checked her boyfriend immediately. I knew an argument would happen, but I couldn't predict what would happen next.

After pressing him, he tried walking out on her. Randy wasn't with the physical games, but my mom was. Also, she had a thing about people leaving her. She wouldn't go for a terminated relationship unless it happened on her terms.

My mom wouldn't let Randy walk out on her that night. When he thought he got away, he had another

Trust Issues

thing coming. That thing coming was a glass jar filled with beads. He was on the edge of the porch with his back turned.

When he turned around to face my fussing and furious mother, she hurled the heavy glass jar at his face. The glass cracked on his face before the ground could crack it. The only time I saw more blood was when I witnessed my cousin's murder. His blood stained the snow and formed multiple puddles.

Everyone was scared to call the ambulance because my mother would probably get a murder charge. The fear of him being dead prompted someone to finally call an ambulance. While they rushed him to the hospital, I wondered if I would ever see him again. Weeks later, Randy returned with several knots and scars covering his head.

CHAPTER 8

It'll Always Be Me & You

While I was supposed to be upstairs, I heard my mother threatening to kill herself and the children inside of her. She was alternating phone lines between a psychic and Randy.

The psychic was telling her that Randy ran off with another woman and he wasn't coming back. My mom pleaded for him to return, or she would kill herself and the twin babies in her womb with a coat hanger.

The surety and desperation my mother put into that statement made me hate wire coat hangers until this day. My sister followed me downstairs when we heard the commotion, but I begged her to go back upstairs. I did my best to protect her from as much as possible and I didn't want her to see our mother in that condition.

I tried stepping as lightly as possible on the carpet steps while I listened to my mother vent suicidal thoughts. The wire hanger was curved into a tool she could potentially use to make her threat a reality.

It'll Always Be Me & You

I started pleading with my mom once she kept voicing her suicidal thoughts. I had never been more fearful of losing my mother. I was willing to do whatever I could to get the hanger away from my mom and help take the pain away. She kept yelling for me to go upstairs while I begged her to not kill herself.

When she could no longer ignore my cries, she told me to come sit next to her. Once I was seated, she wrapped her arms around me, and I could tell that she just needed someone to help her.

My mom smelled like tears and told me her constant pledge, "It'll always be me and you." This situation proved that her pledge was right. I was always the one she could rely on.

CHAPTER 9

He Had It Coming

A couple of months later we were living in a double house. The woman next door had a beautiful daughter in her early twenties. As expressed previously, I was always that nosey kid who had his ear to the streets. I was more interested in what was going on outside instead of what was taking place on TV.

The family next door always used to host a deep crew of Jamaicans. My mom knew most of them from hanging in some project across town. On this particular night, they clouded the neighborhood's atmosphere with weed smoke. The smell that slivered through the window and door seals led me to the front window.

Once the group of Jamaicans stopped smoking, they left the neighborhood. As soon as they turned off the block, the neighbor's boyfriend pulled up.

Kendall, a slender light-skinned guy with a low cut, always caught my attention when he came to the neighborhood. I didn't know what swag was until I saw

He Had It Coming

him. He had the cleanest Cadillac I'd ever seen and jewelry that twinkled like stars on dark ocean water.

I thought this was a casual visit to see the young woman next door. Therefore, I began scanning the neighborhood to see what else was going on. As soon as I looked elsewhere, two cars came flying up the block like they were police with warrants. The Jamaicans returned with a vengeance.

Once they entered the neighbor's house, I heard yelling and bodies getting thrown around. Moments later, Kendall's body was dragged to his Cadillac and beaten lifeless.

By the time my mother rushed to the porch, it was too late to spare Kendall's life. However, it wasn't too late to find out what happened. Before pulling off, one of the killers yelled, "He brought this on himself! He should have known not to put his hands on my daughter!"

CHAPTER 10

Nowhere To Go

Each step during my childhood led me in the wrong direction. I felt things get worse as I got older. The pain from it was deeply rooted in childhood memories that replay vividly when I reflect on them. My grandmother's house was the place to be in the neighborhood, but things spiraled downhill when my mother and I moved there with my siblings.

My mother wasn't fond of my grandparents' relationship. They went through physical battles, but it worked for them. When my mom tried to intervene, my grandmother would tell her, it was none of her business, she couldn't judge what was happening at their house, and she could leave if she didn't like it.

Most fights would start when my grandfather started drinking heavily, as he often did. If he wasn't hallucinating while he was intoxicated, more than likely, he would be into it with my grandmother.

On one occasion, he had to get checked into the hospital because he swore the roof was caving in and

Nowhere To Go

things were crawling out of it. Regardless of my grandfather's vices and struggles, he was deeply loved by many, including me. He was the ideal person to be around when he was sober. My grandfather was a Muslim man who knew how to have a good time and always had wisdom and a good story to share. You would swear he wouldn't harm a fly by his charm, but another side of him came to life when he was intoxicated.

After a fight between my grandparents one night, my mom vocally pressed my grandmother about putting up with the abuse. She yelled, "I am tired of him putting his hands on you!"

I thought another fight was about to happen between them. They were going back and forth about it during the middle of the night. After my grandmother said something my mom didn't like, my mom told my siblings and me to pack our things. My grandmother yelled, "My babies don't have to go nowhere, but you do!"

She yelled back, "Ain't nobody taking my kids from me!"

Nowhere To Go

Initially, I was happy when my grandmother said we could stay, but my happiness was squashed when my mom overrode her and made us leave during the wee hours of the morning.

My mom always told my grandma we had plenty of other places to go. That proved to be untrue when we left the house at 3:00 AM this cold winter morning. We drove all but three blocks.

When my mother saw the disappointment on my face, she coddled me with her speech that it'll always just be me and her. I wished it was me, her, and grandma while I looked in the direction of my grandmother's home and slept in the car for the first time.

CHAPTER 11

My First Crush

It didn't take long for my mother to obtain housing after that incident. I lived in almost every area of the city during my upbringing. That was a gift and a curse. I would establish deeply rooted connections with many people throughout the city, but I wasn't able to nurture those bonds because I moved from place to place.

At this age, I began to focus on impressing girls, but I wasn't taught how. My charm, personality, or looks usually won them over, but I was still rough around the edges.

I wasn't always dressed or groomed appropriately. One girl painfully reminded me of that and gave me a feeling I never wanted to feel again.

Michelle and her family knew me because they lived across the street. Her siblings around our age joked with her every time they saw me and would say things like, "There goes your little boyfriend Moses!" Looking back on it, she took offense to it, but I didn't take heed

My First Crush

of it at the time. I thought she was just playing hard to get.

Michelle didn't even look like she belonged in our hood. It looked like she should have been in Hollywood. She had pure beauty and angelic grace. Nonetheless, Michelle didn't show me much grace when I tried getting at her. I went through extreme measures to show my interest.

It would be fair to say that acts of service have always been my love language. I'd carry her books to school, pick flowers out of people's gardens to give her, and take items out of my house to provide for her in the way I could at the time. She never seemed to be impressed, no matter what I did. I guess one day, she had enough.

On this day, her siblings repeated their favorite line when they saw me - "There goes your little boyfriend, Moses!" I blushed, and she frowned.

She defensively snapped back, "Anh anh! I don't like him!"

That should have been my signal to go home or give my attention to something else, but I did the opposite and tried impressing her. I kept pursuing her because I

My First Crush

thought she felt something when we played spin the bottle a few weeks before, and she entertained my nice gestures.

I was tired of the nice gestures not moving the needle, so I went with my move.

When her siblings went to play elsewhere, I asked, "What do I have to do to make you my girlfriend?"

She put her right hand on her chin and answered, "First, you have to brush your teeth."

I had never visited a dentist's office and didn't have great dental hygiene at the time. I ran into the house and brushed my teeth until my gums bled. I almost scrubbed the yellow and white off my teeth. When I returned, I smiled as if I was posing for a school picture so she could get a whiff of my fresh breath. She replied, "Ok ok. I smell that minty breath."

"What else do I have to do?" I asked as if I were auditioning for a job.

She looked to the sky like her answer was on a teleprompter in the clouds, then said, "You need to comb your hair."

I found an unclaimed bottle of blue S-curl gel in the bathroom at home and rubbed it deeply into my scalp.

My First Crush

This was the most groomed I had been at this age, but I wasn't fully groomed yet. I thought the more groomed I became, the better my chances were to make her my girlfriend. I combed my hair until my scalp became tender, then hurried back to Michelle.

When I returned, I wished she was still looking at the sky because she examined me from head to toe and asked, "Boy, what do you have on? What are you wearing?"

When I realized my outfit wasn't well put together, I ran back inside without saying a word. I knew I had a better outfit hanging up in the closet. My mom had just bought me three outfits. They were purchased for school, but I had a different purpose for them. I was determined to impress my first crush.

My first crush crushed me when she laughed at my outfit and said, "Look at your shoes. They are raggedy!" I was about to run back inside to change. However, those were my only kicks, and no type of shoes would have changed my fate at the time. She continued, "You cool and all, but you ain't even my type. Your teeth all big, and you can't even get it together."

My First Crush

The rest of her judgmental comments sounded like background noise. She got on her high horse and road off once she finished going in on me. I cried myself to sleep that night. I didn't feel good enough and couldn't do anything about it at the moment. Michelle changed the way I carried myself for the rest of my life.

CHAPTER 12

Santa Claus

Christmas came early during one memorable winter. My mom excelled financially when she hung out with my Godmother, Tyrell. There had never been a christening, but that's how she told us to refer to him.

He was one of the most stylish people I ever saw and wore hairstyles like the singing groups, SWV and Escape. Tyrell had outfits that matched his vehicles, chinchilla minks, and jewelry bright enough to light up a dark room.

Tyrell came and went like a rolling stone, but he was consistently around this season. On the first day of December, he showed up at our house and told us Christmas came early.

My Godmother made normal days feel like Christmas. He always showered us with gifts when he came around, so I had huge expectations for this early Christmas. Tyrell instructed my mom to gather the kids and follow him.

Santa Claus

Her partner in crime led us to a hotel where prostitution, drug deals, and corruption went down. After I scoped out the scene, I was no longer worried about the gifts because I became concerned about my surroundings.

It was a dark, foggy night, and the parking lot was filled with sketchy loiterers. I forgot they were there when Tyrell emerged from a hotel room with another man.

They disappeared to the back of the building and then reappeared in U-Haul trucks. The oversized vehicles were filled with bikes, TVs, computers, and toys. When my siblings and I started cheering, Tyrell looked at my mom and gloated, "This is for you and my God kids!" Before he could say another word, several FBI agents drew their weapons and forced Tyrell and the guy he was with to the ground.

CHAPTER 13

The Fire Alarm

I didn't attend school often, but when I was there, mischief was bound to happen. Lunch and recess were integral parts of my childhood. During my second and third-grade years, many meals were missed at home. I am thankful for some of my struggles. They made me resourceful and gave me the instincts to survive anywhere. I became cool with the cafeteria ladies, and they not only looked out for me, but they would look out for my siblings also.

Recess was sacred to me because it was one of the only places my innocence and childhood existed. By the second grade, I experienced more trauma than many senior citizens. I had so much fun one recess that I didn't want to go to class afterward. I always felt that sentiment when it was time to return to class after recess, but this was the first time I concocted the idea to do something about it.

I spoke under my breath and said, "I don't want recess to end." Two of my friends shouted they felt the

The Fire Alarm

same. While everyone in our grade lined up to reenter the building, we devised a plan to stay outside.

Pulling the fire alarm looked like our best bet. I saw the fear in their eyes when we agreed on the plan. I didn't feel any fear, so I volunteered to do it, and they bucked me up to go with my move.

I glided like an undercover agent to the fire alarm, then discreetly pulled it. My friends and I had the laugh of a lifetime when I snuck back by them, and we didn't have to go to our next class. The laughs ended once the fire department, the fire marshal, the ambulance, and the police showed up.

I kept a calm demeanor because my friends were the only ones who knew I pulled the alarm. They were the wrong ones to know. Before I could turn my back, they told the principal I did it.

All it took was for her to make a blanket threat that there would be consequences for the person who pulled the alarm. There were no cameras or other proof that I was the culprit.

Once they provided the principal with proof it was me, she called my grandmother. When she didn't

The Fire Alarm

answer after the third attempt, they pinned a letter on me to inform her about the incident.

Of course, I didn't give it to her. However, that didn't stop her from answering the phone the next day. When I returned home after school, my grandmother and mom were waiting on the porch with belts in their hand. While they left bruises and welts on me, I vowed to never put myself in the situation to be snitched on again.

CHAPTER 14

Suspension

Suspending kids from school isn't always the answer. Should I have been suspended for pulling the fire alarm? Of course. However, I was now in a position to get into even worse trouble outside of school.

My school district was one of the worst in the state. When I think back on it, there was always some other kid to play with in the neighborhood while I was supposed to be at school. The kids who stayed home weren't in any type of rigorous home-school situation. They were home for reasons similar to mine.

While on suspension the day after pulling the fire alarm, I was left home alone with my cousin Barry, who is more like a brother to me. When we were left by ourselves, I knew the trouble I wanted to get into. I didn't view it as trouble at the time, but I know I wouldn't have done the same things if adults were around.

Suspension

On the first day of suspension, I had to go by my Aunt Jackie's house. She stayed in a duplex and had one of the most popular places in the neighborhood. You could easily assume that she was selling drugs out of her house due to the high traffic. People gravitated to her crib because it was always a good time.

There was always a card game, gathering, or cookout at her place. It was mi casa su casa. You could do whatever you wanted at her house, including leaving your kids. That didn't mean they would be watched, but it meant they would be off the streets.

One of the reasons I liked going over there was because of the two pretty girls next door. I was thankful to have them to interact with instead of Michelle. The girls, Barry, and I spent the entire morning playing in the backyard together. Once the sun began draining us, we piled under a tree and entertained each other in various ways. There aren't too many moments of awkward silence among talkative kids.

Once we began cooling off in the shade, we started trying to impress each other. We bragged about the things we'd seen and done that we had no business

Suspension

seeing and doing at that age. All of us had endured some type of childhood trauma. We normalized it because that was our natural environment, and we hadn't experienced anything different. I had already ingested crack cocaine, been molested, and burglarized a place by the age of 8, but had yet to experience my harshest moments of life.

One thing I didn't have experience with was guns. Nonetheless, I told the group of girls that I did when they began bragging about their father's gun. When the sisters said their dad kept it on him at all times, I said I did too. I said it unconvincingly, and the girls didn't believe me. Before they could finish debating, I was headed inside.

I climbed to the top of the refrigerator where my uncle kept his gun in plain sight. The gun looked like it belonged in a video game. It was a chrome revolver with a long nose and a pearl handle.

I didn't know how to hold or handle a gun, but I ran outside with it to show it off to the other children. We had the most dangerous game of show-and-tell while we should have been in school. The girls were impressed by how it looked and how heavy it was. I

Suspension

handled the gun like I was a cowboy in the Wild Wild West to back up my false claim.

Once I finished showing off for them, I hurried inside to put the gun where I found it and repositioned the chair I used. It was impossible to reposition everything. I became out of place mentally when I briefly reflected on the past when I retrieved the crack from the top of the fridge. Also, the excessive dust and oil were obviously tampered with. I shook off the dust bunnies and bad memories, then hurried back outside when I heard someone coming through the front door.

The relief I had when I made it back outside without getting caught gave me the same rush I felt when I pulled the fire alarm. I was confused again when I saw everyone had rushed off. My cousin and the girls were nowhere to be found when I returned outside. They weren't a concern at the moment, so I started playing with the broken fence in the backyard. People walked over it so much that it became a passageway.

The gun was a passageway to my next whipping. I had my head down, digging in the dirt with a stick until my mom snatched me up. My feet were pedaling in the air while she yanked me off the ground by my collar

Suspension

and neck. I was dumbfounded while getting hacked up like I was being thrown out of a club.

Before I was attacked with belts from several directions, my mom yelled, "So you want to go around scaring people with guns huh? You are about to get the whipping of a lifetime!" The girls fabricated what I did with the gun, but my mom didn't fabricate about the whipping I had coming to me. Two women I didn't know, my mom, and grandmom, took turns beating the black off me. I wish I could say that that incident was my most embarrassing beating, but it wasn't.

CHAPTER 15

Everlasting Whippings

Most childhood fights happened over petty reasons. I can recall almost everything in my life, even the small details, but I can't put my finger on why a kid named Bruiser wanted to fight me. His name said it all.

Age differences between adults aren't as significant as childhood age gaps. I was nine years old and several years away from puberty. The guy who wanted to fight me was four years older and had already begun growing facial hair and muscles.

On the second day of suspension, word got out in the neighborhood that he wanted to fight me. Every week, someone in the neighborhood flocked toward a fight. This was the first time I would be a participant in one.

I knew Bruiser wanted to fight me before this, but I strategically avoided him until I couldn't anymore. Moments after I went back inside hiding from him, he

Everlasting Whippings

showed up on our doorstep looking for me. My family inside was confused until it was clear that he wanted to fight me.

When I tried to go upstairs, my mom yelled, "I ain't raising no punk! I don't care what you say. Get your butt out there and fight that boy!" Once I crossed the threshold, it looked like the whole neighborhood was outside. They began cheering Bruiser on as soon as his opponent showed up. For some obnoxious reason, I thought I could talk myself out of the fight or pray it away.

Bruiser pressed me as soon as he saw me. Everything slowed down when he sped up toward me with fire in his eyes and fists balled. When he got within arms' reach, he opened his hands to shove me in the dirt.

I showed minimal resistance, so he kept shoving me. Tears began streaming down my face. I stood there with my fist balled, but was too petrified to use them. I told my mom I didn't know how to fight before stepping inside, and she responded that I would learn today. There had to be a better way.

Everlasting Whippings

Once the shoves were over, a barrage of punches landed squarely on my face. People kept yelling for me to put my hands up and fight back, but doing so wouldn't have kept him off me. I kept looking at my mom to jump in like a boxing referee and stop the fight, but her and no one else watching the fight had plans on stopping it. I got everlasting whippings two days in a row.

CHAPTER 16

Trapped in Trauma

No matter where we moved during my early childhood, we couldn't escape the trauma. Shortly after we moved down the street from my grandmother, my mom got into a heated argument with a man I had never seen before.

My desire to impress other women was rooted in my subconscious because I always saw other men trying to impress my mom. If men weren't pursuing her romantically, they pursued her platonically. She was a big sister and love interest to many. Being tapped in with my mom meant you were connected to almost everyone in town. She was an influencer well before the social media days.

I wasn't worried about my mom while she argued with a man twice her size in our living room. She didn't appear to be concerned about him either. They yelled at each other at the top of their lungs until the man stormed out and slammed the door. I had been around enough at this point to be fearful of retaliation. I

Trapped in Trauma

couldn't believe some of the things they told each other, and I knew the fight wasn't over.

Across the street from our house was a strip mall and a parking lot. That's where the fight continued the next day, but my mom wasn't engaged in the action. Another man who visited us earlier that day crossed paths with the man who disrespected my mother. He got revenge for her once he beat the man unconscious with brass knuckles. My little brother, mom, and I watched the fight from our front steps. Once my mom's enemy was stretched out on the sidewalk, she made us go back inside.

CHAPTER 17

Spike

Have you ever started a day and knew something wasn't right about it? That's how one of the most pivotal days in my life began.

This one started off normal with my mom and her boyfriend fussing, me playing in the yard with my siblings and a few other kids in the neighborhood, and our family dog running around having a better time than all of us.

Spike was a boxer dog that received all of our affection. Every family member held him tight and vented to him whenever we experienced hard times, which was often. Spike was the one soul we could count on to be there for us after a long day or while going through tribulations.

While I was digging into roughly landscaped grass in the side yard, Spike began barking and running in circles. He only did that when danger was near. Danger was nearby often, so I knew something was wrong.

Spike

Once I surveyed my surroundings, I saw unmarked cars circling our residence. They made the block three times. I was worried about a drive-by but knew they weren't looking for any kids. Also, the cars looked too uniform to be executing a drive-by.

Everywhere I turned, I saw a high-level law enforcement officer. I ran inside but couldn't get anyone's attention. I gave up trying to convey what was happening outside and ran upstairs.

Moments after I settled by an upstairs window, the sedans with limo-tinted windows parked in front of my house, and a squad of people wearing bulletproof vests swarmed our house. Our front and back doors were plowed down.

The officers forced everyone onto the ground and made sure everyone in the house was accounted for. They didn't only want my mother, but they wanted her kids. My little brother and sister, and I were escorted to the Child Protective Services Office, and my mom was taken to jail.

My grandmother retrieved us from CPS before any memories could be created there. She questioned us about what happened, but we were too young to

Spike

articulate it. My grandmother was no stranger to raids. Her house set the city record for "most times raided." Therefore, she wasn't too stressed about the traumatic experience. Her calmness rubbed off on me, so I normalized the event at the time.

My mom's quick release helped with normalizing the event. I thought everything would go back to normal, but a few days later, I received confirmation that things would never be the same again. I kept busy at school and the playground over that time, so Spike didn't cross my mind. When I realized he wasn't around, I asked my mother where he was. She sympathetically looked into my eyes and told me that the police killed him during the raid.

CHAPTER 18

Steak and Shrimp

Spike's death caused a lingering, unshakable sadness. Real-life events made me suppress the sadness, and I never had a proper grieving period for him.

I knew my living conditions weren't up to living standards before the state did. We only went to school one-third of the time and were in danger of being dropped from the roll. Most of the time, we missed school because my mom was too tired to bring us, or we could talk our way out of having to go.

Prior to the raid, we lived as if someone was always after us. Apparently, we bounced from place to place mainly because CPS was trying to evaluate our living situation. They had finally cornered my mother and given her strict stipulations that she had to meet in order to keep her kids.

Those stipulations caused a group effort. People I didn't even know were trying to help us get our house in order. Our house smelled like gallons of fabuloso

Steak and Shrimp

and pine sol. The fumes tampered with all our lungs and passageways.

The adjustments weren't all bad. Now, we had TVs in every room, new furniture with plastic wrapped around it, and a refrigerator, pantry, and freezer filled with food. Back then, I couldn't imagine life that good on a regular basis. I knew things were soon to change.

Two days after we got to experience normal living standards, CPS was back at our house. It was far less dramatic this visit. They were there specifically for the children, interviews, and an inspection.

My siblings and I all have different personalities. My sister always told it like it was with no filter. I was the one who had to grow up quickly and had street smarts and survival skills well beyond my years. My little brother was protected from many of the things I had to experience and was coddled by the family and me.

My mom coached us on how to answer the interview questions. Her tutelage worked perfectly for my little brother and me. We answered the questions just how she wanted us to. I told the case worker that we ate steak and shrimp on a regular basis.

Steak and Shrimp

On the contrary, we usually ate ketchup and syrup sandwiches and often missed meals. My little brother didn't go that far, but he covered for my mom at the age of 6 while being interrogated by a seasoned professional.

My sister, on the other hand, told it like it was. She wasn't programmed to lie or run game on someone. Lillian was transparent about what occurred in the household. Instead of taking accountability, my mother took her anger out on the case worker. My stepdad had to restrain her, and that only made our problems worse.

A few days later, the case worker reappeared with a police officer. Our house had already fallen back into worse conditions, and the state was aware of the trauma we were living through. Now, we had to go hide out at my grandmother's house.

CHAPTER 19

Someone Please Call 911

Aside from love, something was always missing in my grandmother's household. If we had electricity, there was no water. If the water was on, the gas and electricity would be off.

It was common to use a bucket of water to flush the toilets or use the buckets as toilets. We used butter knives to protect our household entrances instead of the broken locks on our doors. However, I was thankful for some of our shortcomings.

At the age of 9, I learned how to manipulate the electric box to generate bootleg electricity. The worst flaw of this winter was the cracked window, which made the floors of the house the same temperature as the harsh winter outside. Even though I slept with layers of clothes on, I was still cold.

Using the bucket to use the restroom was what I disliked the most at my grandmother's house. After one occasion, I began preferring that method.

Someone Please Call 911

I always saw my uncle using a bottle to urinate in. Things got gross in the bathroom if someone wasn't tidy with their dealings, and that rarely happened. During this incident, I had to use it badly while I waited in the kitchen for a bathroom or bucket to free up.

When I couldn't wait any longer, I grabbed a bottle from under the sink. After I began urinating, it felt like my private part was on the verge of falling off. When urine touched the ammonia, it exploded and sent me into a tailspin. The rest of the liquid exploded all over the kitchen. Everyone came running into the kitchen, but they didn't know what to do aside from call 911.

CHAPTER 20

The First of The Month

Moving to my grandmother's house gave me a false sense of stability. It was something to get used to but not my desired situation. I didn't have a preferred place to be during this time in my life, but everywhere I went had its own unique form of adversity.

We lived the full hood experience at my grandma's house. Everyone had a role to play in her household. It didn't matter if you were too young to pay bills. My siblings and I were responsible for bringing in the commodity food on Saturday mornings.

The lines to get the government-issued food were longer than the lines to get Jordans on a Saturday morning. All the other kids were there with parents or guardians, and we were there alone for our guardian.

Getting food from here was one of my first conscious recognitions of poverty. I'd be happy to get to the line because I'd be starving, and they would pass out damp, bland, cold-cut sandwiches cut in half.

The First of The Month

When entering the store, we'd be issued two paper bags and permitted to keep what we could carry.

There were several stations. The first one would be the bread. We had to examine it like a food inspector because I commonly spotted mold on the bread that they fed the hood with. People had to be consuming it because each batch of bread had mold, and they'd be emptied by the afternoon.

After the bread section were the eggs, dairy, juice, sandwiches, meat, and desserts, which mostly consisted of Little Debbie cakes. The meat had unsanitary characteristics like the bread, but my grandmother would doctor the meat and serve it to us. We'd be in trouble for not bringing back exactly what she asked for. That probably plays a factor in why I'm able to recall memories so vividly.

On one walk back, I got in trouble for something other than not remembering what my grandmother wanted. Another ulterior motive for going to the store was that my grandmother would let me keep her leftover change after bussing down the food stamps. I commonly spent it on snacks, but this Saturday

The First of The Month

afternoon, I had different intentions for the leftover change.

At this time, I had just heard about smoke bombs. My friend and I linked up after I finished running Saturday morning errands for my grandmother. One week earlier, we heard about smoke bombs and were fascinated by the concept. We were even more excited when we found out the corner store sold them.

Before we ventured to the corner store, my friend encouraged me to get my grandmother's lighter. She knew where everything was in her house and was one of the last people you wanted to upset, so I quickly shot down that idea. I knew there were other people I could have asked for a lighter, but I didn't want to give anyone the power to rat on me if something went down.

I had faith that the friend I was with wouldn't turn on me. We were two peas in a pod when it came to getting in trouble and having each other's back.

The first sentiment proved to be right when he pulled a lighter out of his pocket after we exited the corner store. The employees there knew our parents, so we couldn't expose our plans to do something we

The First of The Month

shouldn't have been doing. That didn't stop him from stealing the lighter.

Once we had what we needed, we sprinted down the block, so we were out of sight of the corner store. After ducking off on a street with a few vacant houses, my friend and I started playing with the smoke bombs.

When I first lit and threw it, we saw flames and smoke. It didn't seem too intense, but I wasn't sure if I did it right. We wanted to see the smoke bomb do more, so I had the genius idea to light the smoke bomb and place it in a large metal mailbox.

Within moments, it started smoking up a storm of black clouds. Once it began rising enough to be seen from a distance, we sprinted in separate directions. Both of us had a few blocks to run. That incident showed me that you can't outrun your problems.

When I returned home, my grandmother asked, "What's wrong, baby?" Before I could catch my breath, and tell her, someone else did. Multiple people appeared on our doorstep. They banged on the door, and when my grandmother opened it, someone yelled, "That little boy blew up our bill money!"

The First of The Month

My grandmother yelled, "Get over here!" When I began walking slowly, she yelled, "Hurry up!"

The fire marshal, firefighters, and several neighbors were on the porch. It was the first of the month, but I didn't know what that meant while putting the smoke bomb in the mailbox. I instantly found out that the first of the month is the time when people commonly pay their most important bills.

Our mailboxes were grouped together with multiple people in the neighborhood. It seemed like all of them were there for my head while they fussed at me. My grandmother knew what she had to do - whip me in front of the neighborhood.

The coldest part about it was that a neighbor passed my grandmother his belt to whip me with. I could tell that all the neighbors wanted to whip me too. They got their satisfaction and enjoyed every strike that lashed my skin.

CHAPTER 21

Broken Appliances

The reason for me bouncing from house to house wasn't always my mother's fault. My grandmother immediately sent me to my aunt's house after the smoke bomb fiasco. Now, my aunt had trouble on her hands. Surprisingly, it didn't have anything to do with me this time.

I don't know what it is about women in my family, but they are aggressive-natured when it comes to making money and confrontation. It was fair to say that my aunt wore the pants in her relationship. She made most of the decisions and often picked arguments with her husband. He'd mostly stand down, but on this day he had enough.

When my aunt tried bossing him around this day, he yelled, "I ain't doing nothing!" When he got that off his chest, my aunt pushed him off the top of the staircase. Her husband went tumbling down the hard steep steps and then landed in the closet at the bottom

Broken Appliances

of the steps. We got the laugh of a lifetime when the closet door slammed behind him.

My family had me demonstrate the incident and how he fell in the closet almost every time he wasn't around. He needed a little time away after that, so I was rolling down the steps often.

It was weirdly constructed, and the door would always slam shut when someone rolled into the closet. My family kept getting a kick out of me rolling down those steps, hurting myself, but it was only a matter of time before they were mad at me again.

My aunt went through so much. Our lives were very much like episodes of Good Times. Almost every time it seemed like we were about to get ahead, adversity happened. I felt bad about adding to her adversity.

One month after the incident with her husband, she hosted a house full of people. My aunt's home wasn't in the ideal condition to host people, but she still had the best house parties and gatherings. Most appliances were broken or on the verge of breaking.

While the adults carried on downstairs, all the kids played hide and seek upstairs. I had always been the

Broken Appliances

competitive type. We didn't have many places, and I didn't want to lose, so I hid in the attic.

Before the party started, my aunt told us not to break anything. Her request would go unfulfilled. This time I got tricked into breaking the rules.

While playing in the attic, my sister and cousin told me to stay on the boards. The board was my only passageway to hide successfully. I started smiling once I started bear crawling, but there wasn't a smile in the house when all my weight on the board caused the ceiling to collapse.

I landed lower back first on my cousin's bed downstairs. My head was inches away from his hardwood dressers. I wouldn't be here or competent enough to tell my story if the back of my head had collided with his dresser.

Several people downstairs frantically yelled, "What's that!" The greatest actor in the world couldn't have acted like they were asleep after falling through the roof. Nonetheless, that's what I did when my aunt barged into the room.

Before I could feel the pain of the contusions, the pink insulation caused my skin to feel like it was on fire.

Broken Appliances

Until this day, I have yet to feel an itch that bad. Drywall, upholstery, and insulation were all over my cousin's room, along with remnants from the ceiling and roof. When my smile turned into helpless cries, my aunt yelled, "I know this boy did not just cave my ceiling in! Everybody get out right now!"

CHAPTER 22

Hit & Run

When street activities occurred inside, the adults would tell the kids to go outside. It's crazy how being outside was sometimes safer than what was taking place inside. However, that wasn't the case this day.

My grandmother told us to play outside while my uncle sat on the porch. More than likely, he was sitting there as a lookout instead of a babysitter. Once I went outside, my cousin asked if I wanted to play catch. My aunt was the last person to go inside. She instructed us not to go in the street.

We lived on a busy street with a few lanes and a narrow curb. Cops could write speeding tickets all day in this area. I had knowledge of this, but I still ran into the street to get the football when it was overthrown.

Looking both ways before crossing the street wasn't a thing for me back then. My aunt ran outside to get something out of the car. When she saw me weaving

Hit & Run

through traffic to get the ball, she yelled, "Didn't I tell y'all stay out the street!"

I paid her no mind when I threw the football back to my cousin. She shook her head and then started talking to my uncle. On the next throw, I wondered if my cousin intentionally overthrew the ball. It was always funny when my aunt threw a tantrum.

She used to talk with a cigarette hanging off her lips and pointed when she talked. I didn't want to hear her fuss at me again. So, I sprinted to get the football.

Our front yard was a hill. When we ran up it, we faced resistance. When he ran down it, we had plenty of momentum. That momentum propelled me into the street. Consequently, I was clipped by a car with a driver hurrying to get somewhere. Not only was he driving above the speed limit, but he didn't have the humanity to check to see if I was alive or to take accountability.

Several recollections happened between when I heard my cousin and grandma yell, "No!" and when I woke up in the hospital. I blacked out after I locked eyes with the driver, and he plowed through me.

Hit & Run

Once I regained consciousness, I began wondering what happened with the football. The ambulance being on the scene spoke to how long I was knocked out. Almost everyone in the neighborhood was crowded around me while they were concerned about my well-being. I woke up to frantic faces and my family members hugging each other and praying.

Despite their concern, I didn't feel any. I was rushed to the hospital. I had been struck by a car and propelled in the air high enough to dunk a basketball.

Somehow, I landed on the pavement but only ended up with war wounds I could brag about. I vowed to look both ways every time I crossed the street going forward. Looking back on it, God always had me covered during the most dangerous times.

CHAPTER 23

LA Gears

Not learning from my mistakes caused me to learn an abundance of lessons during my early childhood. I knew to look both ways but still didn't listen or avoid trouble.

Jordans weren't the only shoes of this era. LA Gears had quite the run in the late 1980s and early 1990s. Kids' statuses in the neighborhood, at school, and on the playground skyrocketed if they had a pair. I begged my mom for a pair once I realized I could ascend the social hierarchy.

I asked my grandmother first because I knew I had a better chance with her. She flat-out told me no. My mom was hit-or-miss when it came to buying me what I wanted. Her income was up and down.

When it was up, she showered us with material items, but other than that, we were deprived. I couldn't settle for the deprivation of the LA Gears. That is what she tried to make me do when she shouted, "Boy, ain't nobody wasting their money on those!"

LA Gears

I knew there was no chance of her buying the shoes even though she claimed she'd try to once she felt bad about shutting me down in that manner. I knew I'd have to get it how I lived.

Getting it how you live occasionally influences a person to get it how they see others living. I saw multiple family members finesse shoe stores by trying on a new pair of shoes and walking out in them. I didn't know if they did any steps in between, but knowing how they got the shoes they wanted gave me an idea.

I almost started hating the mall when I went there with my great aunt, mom, and grandma. We stopped at almost every store, and they tried on something in most of the stores they went into. My mom told me she would buy me the shoes one day, but obviously, she didn't mean today.

She shut me down again quickly when I asked her if she could purchase the shoes. I was strategic when I asked, too. I waited until I saw that she had enough cash to buy the LA Gears. My mom had enough money plus more, but she still told me no.

This was a prime example of not accepting no, for an answer. It felt like an insult to injury when my family

LA Gears

went into a store that sold LA Gears, and no one had intentions of buying me the kicks I desperately wanted.

My plan for the shoe heist couldn't go according to plan because the LA Gears lit up when you walked. It was like trying to commit an armed robbery in broad daylight wearing a yellow hoody.

Walking out there in stolen light-up shoes may have been the wildest thing I could have done. I didn't do it, but I did the second craziest thing I could have done in this scenario.

After trying the shoes on, I tucked them under my jacket until my family was ready to leave the store. One employee began watching me the moment I asked to try on the LA Gears. We had made eye contact several times during my heist, but that didn't stop me.

The alarm started beeping as soon as I crossed the threshold of the store. Most people from the hood are prone to getting profiled, so my family went left field when they tried to accuse them of stealing. I don't know what kept the employee from exposing me. She could have easily made me open my jacket and got me in serious trouble.

LA Gears

I didn't need her to rat on me because I did it myself. My family complained about the lady during the whole walk to the car. Because of that, I didn't think there was any way they would side with her over me. Once I conceptualized that, my aunt yelled, "Why is she mad at us?"

Even though my aunt said it rhetorically, I innocently answered, "Probably because I stole their LA Gears!"

My mom took her eyes off the road and pulled over. Once the car was in park, they took turns whipping me. This was a painful lesson I learned from. I never stole again.

CHAPTER 24

Flesh & Blood

Blood is thicker than water, but thinner than stacks of money. The almighty dollar has influenced people to turn on their best friends and immediate family members. If I didn't know my aunt's and mother's family history, I wouldn't have known they were related during this life-changing occurrence.

A $5,000 money order that belonged to my mother went missing, but I couldn't believe that one of my aunts would steal from their own sibling. As much as I wanted to believe my aunt didn't take it, there was overwhelming proof she stole it.

My mom rallied a gang of people, including me, to confront my aunt. This family business would be on the streets. Everyone in the hood knew where my aunt hung out. Her stomping grounds were at a complex down the street from where we lived. It felt like we were in a movie while we stormed the streets looking for her.

Flesh & Blood

Some people pled for my mother to stop. Several others ran ahead to warn my aunt of the wrath heading her way. Several instigators were thirsty to watch two sisters fight each other. I walked with my mother militantly, but I was fearful for my aunt.

When we turned onto her street, my aunt ran inside. My mom took off running when she spotted her sister. My aunt was behind closed doors by the time my mother was down the block, but that didn't stop my mom.

She banged on the door until it was about to come off the hinges. The threat to kick the door down forced her to come outside. My mom had heavy hands and punched through things, including my aunt. Once my mom beat her sister to the ground, she started dragging her and reminded people of what would happen if they crossed her.

My family fighting each other in front of the neighborhood changed my temperament and the temperature. It was a hot and gloomy day, but it turned cold as I watched my mom strangle my aunt with an extension cord. I wished I could have replaced the money order my aunt stole.

Flesh & Blood

If I didn't know to stop stealing after the mall incident, I knew not to steal after this one. I saw death in my aunt's eyes while her sister strangled the life out of her and demanded the money she stole from her. My mom looked into her sister's dilapidated eyes and yelled, "I don't care about killing you! You don't care about stealing from me!"

My mom spared her sister's life after she collapsed. It was traumatizing to watch family members steal from each other and go to war over money. I always feared my mom, and this incident was one of the reasons.

CHAPTER 25

Fork in The Road

Just because I quit stealing didn't mean I was done wearing stolen merchandise. My grandmother hid my confiscated LA Gears in a TV stand that didn't have a television. I let two days go by, then made plans for the shoes.

I took the shoes with me to school but not on my feet. I waited until I entered the school to put them on. When my friends first saw me wearing the LA Gears, they shouted, "Wow, he really got the shoes! That boy got money!"

My popularity skyrocketed, and I took extensive measures to keep wearing the shoes until they wore out. The hood was filled with a lot of broke people trying to look rich for other broke people. Even the kids had a backward mentality.

The longest measure I went through to wear the shoes happened on a day that changed my life forever. There were two paths to school. A ten-minute walk with a clean path on a sidewalk or a dirty path that cut

Fork in The Road

through fields, potholes, a trailer park, and unkept neighborhoods. Your shoes were bound to get dirty walking that path. I was responsible for waking my siblings up and walking them to school. My mom made me accountable for them. We were all motivated to make it to school early every day. There was no breakfast at home, but we received free breakfast in the cafeteria.

This day, we were late and hurrying, so the shortcut was the only option to make breakfast. I didn't have time to hide the shoes either. Therefore, I wrapped them in bags before we started walking to school on this dark, cold, and damp winter morning. I almost slipped every step of the way to school, but we still made it in time for breakfast. Making it to breakfast while we were starving and had given up hope made it seem like it would be a great day.

My day started perfectly. We were late, but the secretary administered us hall passes to class, and we had full stomachs. Plus, I had extra snacks in my bag and was enjoying the attention from my LA Gears.

When I got bored in a class before lunch, I asked to be excused for the restroom. I had no intention of

Fork in The Road

relieving myself. I just wanted to lurk the hallways. My sister's class was next to mine, so I stopped there first. I didn't see her in the first few rows, but I saw my little brother in the first row of his class. The smile on his face warmed my heart and became forever indented in my memory.

After killing time in the hallways, I knew I wouldn't be able to be excused for the restroom again, so I relieved myself while I had the chance to. It was strange not to see my sister at recess or throughout the day, but I didn't question it until she was nowhere to be found after school.

My brother and I stood by the doors waiting for her until a few hours after school ended, and all the custodians were leaving the building. One teacher was the only faculty member left in the building. She was as concerned as my brother and I when we told her our sister was missing.

We checked every restroom stall, janitor closet, and classroom throughout the entire school. All of us checked the building so thoroughly that we knew for sure she wasn't on the premises. I was petrified for two reasons - I knew my mom would whip me for losing

Fork in The Road

track of my sister, and I was fearful of what happened to her.

I didn't know if I should walk home slowly or hurry. The situation appeared to be a catch-22 and double trouble. Something would be wrong either way. We lollygagged home because I knew I was going to get a whipping.

Sometimes, our biggest fears should be the least of our concerns. In retrospect, I should have run home. I had a justified reason other than the selfish one. I thought I kept hearing her voice on the walk home, but I realized it was an illusion once we reached our residence at 7:00 PM, and she was still nowhere to be found.

When I gave my mom the news, she began cursing up a storm. She continually yelled at me, asking, "How did you lose your sister?" The attention was off me when my mom realized I had already exhausted all options to find her.

She called every branch of law enforcement to help locate my sister. Before I knew it, helicopters and police officers were on the task of looking for my sister. The following day, CPS called to inform my mom that

Fork in The Road

they had my sister, and they were coming for the rest of her kids.

The legal kidnapping made us end the standoff with CPS. They took someone valuable from us. Now, we had to comply with their demands.

My grandmother begged for custody of us when we arrived at the CPS building. We were happy to see my sister, but my happiness was short-lived. There was nothing my mom could say to help our case. They had already tried enforcing their stipulations, but she didn't comply.

Sometimes, we don't know how badly we are missing something until we need it. My sister's father and my brother's dad showed up for them, but I didn't have a daddy to show up for me. Therefore, I became state property and was forced into foster care.

Made in the USA
Middletown, DE
12 July 2024